Thoughts
from a
Teenager's Mind

Chad Gerald Crump

ISBN 979-8-89243-310-5 (paperback)
ISBN 979-8-89243-311-2 (digital)

Christian Faith Publishing
832 Park Avenue
Meadville, PA 16335
www.christianfaithpublishing.com

Printed in the United States of America

These days, when you buy a book of poetry, it is usually written by older people, and it is written about their life experiences. I thought it would be nice to read something different.

These days, when you hear the word *teenager*, you think about uncontrollable troublemakers, wild kids out of control. But we are not that way. And everyone sometimes in their life was and will be a teenager. So I thought it would be nice to read what a teenager thinks about.

I have expressed what I think in poetry. I consider myself an average teenager. I am going through my teen years right now, so I know what it is like to be a teenager right now. We have more things now than our parents did when they were teenagers, and so will our children have more than us. But at this time in my life these are the things I thought about and things I saw and felt.

I hope you like these poems and understand and/or remember that the teenage years are hard. Your entire world is changing, you are changing. And this is some of my journey.

Chad Gerald Crump

TEENAGER'S AGE

You walk the streets at night
As the devil keeps you in his sights.
You walk the line between right and wrong.
One false move, and you're gone.
So many choices to make.
Which one, which one should you take.
Life is so hard when you or our age.
So many wars we must engage.

MY THREE BUTTERFLIES

My three butterflies as precious as a time of old.

One is my eyes that can pierce the soul. Exposing the world and all its diamonds and gold.

One is my passion, fierce and bold, the blood that races through my veins. And all the love my heart can hold.

The other is my strength, my protection. My blanket of comfort when I am cold.

Beauty beyond perfection, bound by an unbreakable connection.

My three butterflies as precious as a time of old.

A LONELY MAN

A rose's scent throughout the air
Brings sweet memories of a love no longer there.
A cool autumn breeze, flowing across the land,
Brings tears to a lonely man.
Blue, a deep blue the sky rejects.
But gray is all that it reflects.
A darkened heart in a darkened world,
All for the loss of a young beautiful girl.
Dreams of angels, flight they take,
And with them they steal the heartache.
Flowers, a million colors, die at one touch,
From the coldness of a man who once loved so much.
Through all the pain and sorrow, he keeps his head
    held high
For the opportunity to once again fly,
With faith that his heart will mend, and he will expe-
    rience love once again.

TIST TASK

"Tist tist, task task," said the man behind the mask.

"Tisk tisk, task task, what do you mean?" I asked to the man behind the mask. But no reply that I received, he just smiled with ease.

"Tist tist, task task," I asked once more to the man behind the mask. But he said nothing to me, just grinned with ease.

I was getting angry. Inside me was burning red fire of anger. I said, "You come up to me and say, 'Tist tist, task task,' but you won't take off the mask.

"You just smile, knowing I'm mad. You won't answer me, but making me mad just seems to make you glad. So I'll ask, just one time more. If no answer, I will raise my hands to score."

To the man behind the mask, "What do you mean, saying, 'Tist tist, task task'?"

The man behind the mask grinned and said only these four undreamed words. That has made my curiosity aroused and has made my anger announced. Now he stands before me with this shiny black velvet mask and says, "Tist tist, task task."

With all my heart and soul, I truly hate the unknown man behind the mask.

WHY WON'T YOU LOOK MY WAY?

Why won't you look my way? Look into my eyes, it's a great love. A love for you, I cannot deny. You don't give me a time of day, no matter what I do or say. I love you, but I'm too shy to tell you. You might laugh dead in my face for what I would say to you. I see you every day, and I ask, "Why won't you look my way?"

Your hair is gorgeous, your eyes are lovely as the sky. If I can't have you, I think I would rather die. I admire you, but you will never know. Because I am nothing but a raven or a black crow. Watching you, staring at you, dreaming of you. I see you every day, and I ask, "Why won't you look my way?"

My heart pumps thoughts into my head, not of talking but of walking and holding hands instead. I dream of you at night, of me holding you tight. I could give you a wonderful love. I think you were sent from above. Beautiful as a dove, flying in the air. How can I dare to even look at you standing over there. I see you every day and I ask, "Why won't you look my way?"

I would like to think heaven has sent you, as lovely as you are. As beautiful and soft as you may be. I think hell sent you to tempt me. I can't hold you and caress you gently. Hell has sent you to torture me. Heaven sent you for me to see every day, and I ask, "Why won't you look my way?"

One look from you would make me weak, one kiss from you would make my heart weep. One smile from you would make my defenses fall. One touch from you would make the snow thaw. I see you every day and ask, "Why won't you look my way?"

I would treat you like a queen; I will give you everything. You're more beautiful than the flowers in the woods. I would love you forever if I could. Only if you would.

YOU MEAN TO ME

There she is, yes, the one I love. Over there, showing me what beautiful is made of.

I'm going to tell her how I feel. And if I must, I will let my heart spill.

But what will I say? Maybe I will think about it for a day.

No, I must tell her now!

But how? When I'm around her, I can't make a sound.

She's so beautiful. What would she want with me?

God, I want her, mine to be.

Girl, can't you see? Can't you see how much you mean to me?

Little, little old me. Can't you see? Please look at me.

I want you to see. How much, just how much.

You mean to me.

SUDDEN DEATH

I plunged the knife in the skin. I did it again and
  again.
This man won't die, he won't even cry. He sits there
  and looks at me.
An evil look, and I knew he could see. See just how
  scared I am of him.
I took his bloody body and sat him in the corner. I lit
  my cigarette, and I sat down on the bed.
I took a good look at him. I was wrong. This man is
  dead.
My task was but half over. This murder I must cover.
I must conceal what I have done.
Because they will arrest me with murder ONE.

ONE SINGLE TEAR

In this darkened room all alone, sitting in front of the fire. Every time the wood cracks a sound, it sends a chill to my bone. Sitting, staring, sympathizing with my fear. Down my pale face ran one tiny, wet, salty tear.

I hear every little, insignificant sound. There is horror all around. So I sit very still and watch the flames of the fire. I watched them dance at will. Little demons playing in the flames. Just playing the devil's games. On my mind is everything, but if I think about it, in my mind, there's nothing. But still again, a little tear runs down my face.

The shadows on the floor slightly moved to form something totally new. A chill ran from my head to my feet. And any thoughts of hope in my mind have admitted defeat. My fingertips have gone numb. I wish, I wish there was somewhere to run. But I can't escape, escape this fear inside. So I sit here in the room, this dark, black room of horror and gloom. And let only that one tear fall.

The moon is out, and the stars are bright. But their light will not shine in my room tonight. I would sleep, but I'm afraid that I wouldn't wake. But for God's sake, for heaven's sake. Won't tomorrow ever come? But only that tear falls, yes, only that one.

The fire has thrown its light upon the wall. Oh, how my hopes of life I can barely recall. My eyes are pale and my heart is weak. I can hear the boards in the floor in the hall. I can hear them creak. I feel my inside start to rise, as if, as if I was about to die. But I'm not. I'm not going to die, and I won't cry, except for this one single tear.

But in this room, all alone, because my beloved one is gone. I wish something would come along and take my life away. I wish I could be dead today. But death walks my house day and night. It took my wife, but it won't take my life. I look death in the eyes, and it grins at my hurt. Yet taking my life it seems to avert. But I might be dead, and this is hell. But hell couldn't hurt this well. Please, Death, take me away. I can't stand this dark room and this single tear another day.

BULLDOG

Little old dog, looking bad. You look like someone
    had made you mad.
You growl and you bark when we take you to the
    park.
You're small but you're stout, you are little, so we
    must watch you when you're out.
Little bulldog, you're rough and you're tough. When
    others see you, they think you want to fight.
But they don't know your bark is worse than your
    bite.

SUMMER SCHOOL

Sleepy, sleepy, sleep. I need to get up, I need to get
out of bed.
My body's so tired, I feel like I'm dead.
Just a few more minutes, that's all I ask. Getting up,
that's a tough task.
I want to sleep just a little more. When I yawn, it
sounds like a lion's roar.
I'll get up now, even though I don't want to. I say to
myself, "Get up, you."
I must be a fool. I've got to get up and go to summer
school.

ANOTHER DRINK

Another drink, please. Don't ask questions, just give the drink to me.

I'm sorry I screamed, but it seems my life is a bad dream.

I think I need another shot. Come on, one more should hit the spot.

I hate that woman you see. Oh God, give the bottle to me.

I was wrong, I don't hate her. The truth is I love her.

Bartender, I think I want something stronger. I can't take this memory any longer.

I went home, and that woman, she was, she was gone. Is that the strongest you got? Here, fill my glass up to the top.

What? I'm going to drink myself to death. Well, if I die, tell everyone that I was drinking when I left.

You don't understand, I was once a great man. I've got plenty of money, so give me another round. Give me another cigarette, mine fell on the ground.

What? This drink is from the lady at the end of the bar. What does she look like? I can't see that far.

Well, bartender, I'm going down that road again. Do you think this is a sin?

Hi, beautiful, my name is Ace. Bartender, another drink please, that woman I met the other day. Has splattered my heart all over the place.

Another drink and fast, I want this memory to hurry up and pass.

LET HER KNOW

She kept you through all the pain. She did it with
 nothing to gain.
You want to treat her bad, man, you must be insane.
She loves you more than you know. If you love her,
 let her know.
Please don't put on a show. Let her know now.
Before it's too late. Before she is beyond the pearly
 gates.
When you can only see her in your dreams and hear
 her in your young babies' screams.
Tell her before she is dead and gone away. Go tell her
 now, right away.
Don't delay, tell her. Let her know today (I love you,
 Mom).

IT'S THE PEOPLE THAT MADE US FALL

I walked down the street. I can't believe what I see. People in cardboard boxes, begging me. "Please, any spare change?" These people seem to have nothing to gain.

I walked down the street. I can't believe what I see. Big white houses with picket fences. People driving Mercedes-Benzes. What kind of world is this? It's not the world at all. It's the people that made us fall.

Down the road, I hear a gunshot, and I hear a car speed away. I think to myself, *Someone else must have just died in a bad way.* Money has corrupted people these days. People steal from their mothers. Commit murder on others. What kind of world is this? It's not the world at all. It's the people that made us fall.

Every day, someone dies. Every day, a liar denies. Every day, a politician lies. Every day, we say good-bye. What kind of world is this? It's not the world at all. It's the people who made us fall.

FRIENDS ARE THERE

Friends are there when times are tough.
Friends are there when this world really gets rough.
Friends are good to have.
Friends are there when you get depressed and sad.
Friends are there in times of need.
So heed the words that I say, "If you need a friend,
  you can always come my way."

OUT SHAGGING

Out on the floor, shagging, what a sensation. Out shagging to the temptations.

The beach music is playing loud. Out shagging with the crowd.

Your partner in your arms, your feet are moving on the floor. Trust me when you're out shagging, it's not a bore.

Pack your things up, tell your friends goodbye. When they ask why.

Say, "I'm going to Myrtle Beach to do the electric slide."

The tunes are spinning. The embers are singing.

You're not dreaming, you're out shagging.

It does not matter the cost. As long as you get to do the boss.

The floor is slick and your shoes are shined. You're out shagging and wiggling you're behind.

Someone says, "Hey, that's old." You say, "Get out of my way, I'm out shagging today."

MY THANK-YOU LETTER

Thank you for the world that we live on.
Thank you for the birds that sing their song.
Thank you for the land and sea.
Thank you for the sky and air.
Oh, how could we dare to even destroy these things?
Thank you for my friends.
Thank you for my many happy grins.
Thank you for my parents, especially my father's wife.
Thank you for my life.
Thank you for winter, summer, fall, and spring.
Dear GOD, I want to thank you; thank you for
    everything.

GOODBYE

In the blink of an eye, you were gone.
With no warning, without even a so long.
I love you so much.
But I didn't know love could hurt such.
I dream about you.
Why couldn't you have been true?
Why did you have to make me feel so blue?
I miss your kiss and your tender touch,
I miss it so, so very much.
Sometimes I miss you so much I cry.
Why couldn't you have just said goodbye?

WHERE IS MY LIFE?

Where's my life? Between my work and school. I feel tired and strife. Girls come and go.

Where's my life? I don't know.

Where's my life? I'm always on the go. I never can stop. I'm only a teenager. But I move so much. I feel like I'm going to drop. I go through rain and snow.

Where's my life? I don't know.

Where's my life? I can't find love. I have had plenty of girls, but they all seem to leave. And sometimes I do grieve. To them, I never had enough. I'll tell you, this teenage boy has it rough. It seems all the girls I like just go.

Where's my life? I don't know.

Where's my life? I study hard at school. Then I go straight to work. And sometimes I do like to flirt. My parents always getting on me. Keeping me straight, you see.

Where's my life? I don't know.

Where's my life? I'm not strung out on drugs. I do the best I can. I'm trying to become a man. I am not a teenage father. I push myself to be smarter and work harder.

So where is my life?

Right here. It's not the greatest. But I'm trying to live it to the fullest.

MOM

You call her Mom.
For you, she has been loving, fierce, strong, patient,
 and calm.
Sometimes she gets on to you, punishes you for doing
 bad stuff.
But in the end, you love her so much.
She is the truest friend that there will ever be.
You wait and see.
She will be there when you are happy and comfort
 you when you are sad.
Please, don't hurt her or make her mad.
Be proud and glad.
Of the MOTHER that you have.

THE WEATHER

The snow is lying thick on the ground.
It is a white blanket lying all around.
What was green is not anymore.
What was beautiful is covered with white snow, and
 the wind whistles a chilling score.
Seasons changes. The world does too.
When the weather changes, something changes in
 me and you.
When the air gets cooler, the human heart gets
 warmer.
When the temperature gets colder, people get nicer.
The snow is white, cold, covered over the ground.
It is a white blanket lying all around.

DARKNESS

Solid, black cloth of darkness.
Seems to cover your whole world, and it feels so
    heartless.
What you saw, you see no more.
What you hear, you hear no more.
What you thought, you cannot think no more.
This cloud of darkness cleans your mind, and it
    opens a new door.
The door to fear, to your greatest, terrifying fears.
You feel your eyes fill up with tears.
When the darkness comes, you find that you are all
    alone.
And all light of any strength is gone.
Beyond death, beyond sleep.
You feel your feet fall deep.
Deeper into the darkness. The darkness swallows you
    whole.
It seems you fall, fall, fall, deeper, deeper, deeper in
    the hole.

You have no idea what to do.
You are too scared to move.
Then the light comes and breaks through the
darkness.
Destroying it with its brightness.
The bright, white light turns your expression to a
grin.
Yes, you have found love again.

THE WEAKEST

My hands are rough and tough.
But they did not get to hold you enough.
My arms are strong, and my muscles are too.
But with all my strength, I couldn't hold on to you.
My memory is stubborn and it keeps remembering
     you.
And every time it does, my tough feelings turn blue.
My eyes may have perfect sight.
But the tears made them blurry that night.
My wits are sharp and my mind is smart.
But my heart.
Well, my heart is the weakest, and I think you knew.
Because you broke it in two.

IF THE WALLS COULD TALK

If the walls could talk.
If only there was a way.
I would sit and listen every day.
Love, hate, evil, good.
Only if they could.
Only if the walls could talk.
What would they teach us about?
Would they spill it all out?
What would they say
If they could talk for one day?
Could they tell us about the past and the future too?
If only they could talk to me and you.
What could they tell?
Death, suicide, murder, pleasures of heaven, or tor-
    tures of hell.
Oh, what would they tell?
Their words would sail like a hawk.
If only the walls could talk.

MY GUIDE

The stars are not shining brightly.
I do not take this lightly.
I need them to guide me through night and day.
I let them lead me on my way.
Through love and life, I watched them every night.
But for some reason, they are not out tonight.
What will I do? The moon is gone too.
I need help, I need my star. My light from afar.
I need them to show my way.
Wherever they have led me, they have never led me
    astray.
They have never been wrong.
And always shined strong.
Where are you tonight? You are totally out of sight.
Oh no, what a fright. The stars are not shining
    tonight.

TIME FOR BED

My eyes were getting heavy.
I'm getting sleepy. My skin is getting creepy.
My strength has failed. And my confidence has
    bailed.
My legs are wobbly. I can stand, hardly.
I can't keep my eyes open. I feel like I'm choking.
My back hurts, my head aches. And my poor hands
    have the shakes.
My bed is so warm. I'm lying in perfect form.
Won't be long until I'm dreaming. If I don't go to
    sleep fast, I'll be screaming.
I toss and turn all night long. How many times have
    I heard this song?
I finally go to sleep to wake and find out I was never
    in bed. I dozed off on the couch instead.
My body goes numb from my feet to my head. I
    think it's time to go to bed.

ABOUT THE AUTHOR

The author is a young teenager, just starting to express himself in his writing. The subjects are from external experiences. Being young, his world is still small and protected. He is just beginning to use the craft of writing and fine-tuning his God-given gifts.